www.FlowerpotPress.com
PAB-0808-0324
Made in China/Fabriqué en Chine

POLAR PALS

James Roberts

This is an ARCTIC HARE.

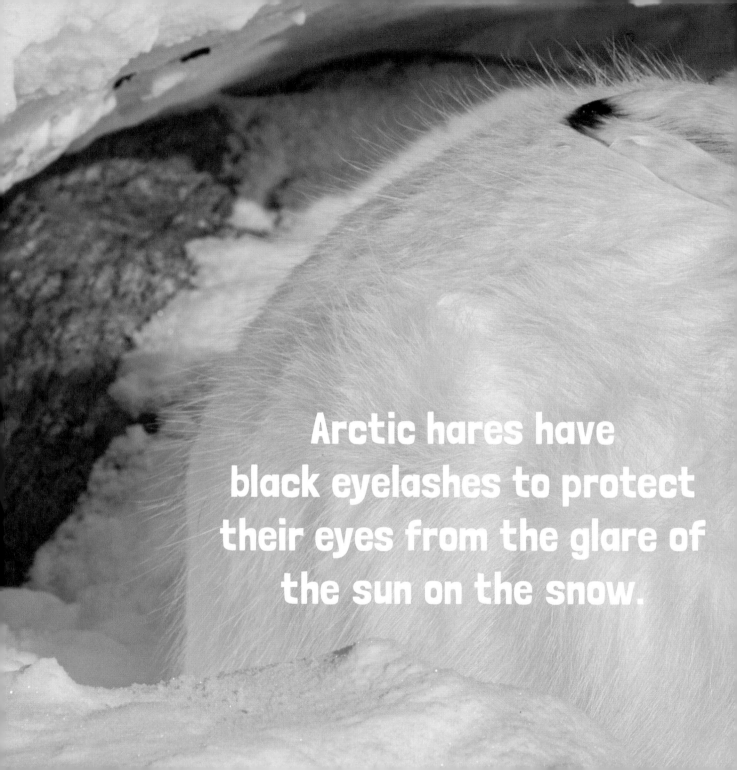

Arctic hares have
black eyelashes to protect
their eyes from the glare of
the sun on the snow.

This is a GYRFALCON.

Gyrfalcons are the largest falcons in the world and one of the most fierce predators in the Arctic.

This is an ARCTIC FOX.

Arctic foxes change the color of their fur depending on the season. It is brown in the summer and white in the winter.

This is a POLAR BEAR.

Polar bears have big, furry paws that help them walk on ice and snow.

This is a FUR SEAL.

Fur seals have a thick layer of blubber and extra fur to keep them warm in their cold habitat.

This is a PTARMIGAN.

Ptarmigans often burrow
in the snow during winter
as a way to camouflage
themselves from predators.

This is a
KING PENGUIN.

King penguins gather together in big groups called colonies.